Seeking Courage

*Inspirational quotations
to give you encouragement*

Lorna Arthur

Lorna Arthur works in a career information library where each day she meets people of all ages and religions who are seeking to build a meaningful life. She also spent six years teaching faith and values to teenagers at a Christian school in Perth.

Although Lorna was born and studied in England, she now lives in the capital city of Australia, Canberra. She enjoys writing and meeting new people, and is married with two teenage sons.

Her first book, **Rocky Road**, contains stories and parables about the Christian life. This and her books of inspirational quotations **Seeking God**, and **Seeking Understanding**, can all be ordered through Autumn House.

First published in 2006
Copyright © 2006
All rights reserved. No part of this publication
may be reproduced in any form without prior
permission from the publisher.
British Library Cataloguing in Publication Data.
A catalogue record for this book is available
from the British Library.

ISBN 1-903921-35-X

Published by Autumn House
Grantham, England.
Printed in Thailand

Seeking Courage

*Inspirational quotations
to give you encouragement*

Lorna Arthur

Dedicated with much love to to our son Lindley

Ten Cents of Courage

As you hold this small book in your hand do you feel full of courage, or are you almost on empty?

The title springs from an experiment I once devised when I felt particularly low on courage.

To become more motivated to take on life's challenges I decided to pay myself for being courageous.

As I live in Australia, and we use dollars and cents, I went to the bank and bought a bag of 10 cent coins. I took the bag home and found a clear jar and carefully cut a small slit in the lid. Then, whenever I did something courageous, however small it seemed, I paid myself 10 cents.

At first it was slow going as everywhere I looked there seemed to be more work than I could handle. But gradually I gained momentum. I attacked the messy kitchen, and dish by dish brought it to order, so I paid myself 10 cents. Then I made a difficult phone call, and did the same. Soon it became a game, and after I had written letters, swept up the leaves, or cleaned up the garage, I rewarded myself. Soon the full jar was testament to my courage, the courage I thought I had lost forever.

It was just a small experiment, but I came to realise that to live courageously does not mean slaying dragons or saving maidens. It often means just facing the small dragons of daily life. Although it may sometimes mean saving others, at a deeper level it can also mean saving ourselves.

Blessings!

Lorna

Acceptance

The first action of courage may be to face things that cannot be changed.

To deny something is to lie about it, and to base your life on very shaky foundations. To accept something is to know the parameters of its truth, and to know where you can stand, and where you can build.

Who you are

I crave the same thing as
my enemy, my parent and
my child – to be accepted
for who I am.

A child born to a single
parent does not need
a half-hearted welcome
but double the welcome
and love.

Where you are

Pragmatism accepts reality
as it is, and bows to it. Idealism
sees all that can be changed, and
works towards it. Sanity lies
somewhere in between.

Acceptance is a form
of pragmatic honesty.

Action

Most of us are reactive. We wait for circumstances, or other people, to cause a stimulus, then we scramble to respond. This means that our strings are constantly pulled by someone else, and we angrily bob around like powerless puppets.

But we can choose to be proactive, to anticipate events, to lead out in our own lives.

Inner fire

Life is not just about running
around putting out the fires
lit by emotional arsonists.
Life is also about acting
upon our own inner fire.

Adventure

We are willing to be adventurous in one area in direct proportion to our sense of security in others.

Christians should be willing to ask new questions, forge new trails and to go to the ends of the earth, because their security is in a loving and unchanging God.

Choose!

Whether we choose to stay in our armchair or sail the seven seas, we are still risking our lives.

Autonomy

Is the wind a threat to the
eagle's flight or does it enable it?
Is the Spirit of God really
a threat to yours?

People, like cars,
need to be self-starters.

Beginners

The world is full of beginners.
This is the first time for all of
us.

Whatever your dream,
may you have the courage
to start, the tenacity to see it
through and a sense of a job
well done when it is completed.
In other words, may your life be
blessed and be a blessing.

Boasting

I boast in order to convince
myself, as well as to convince
you.

The louder I shout,
the more I fear self-doubt.

Boundaries

If people walked all over your
land you would build a fence,
or call in a contractor to
help you build it.
If people walk all over you,
build an emotional fence,
or call on a counsellor
to help you build it.

Know your limits

Although I would love to
help the world,
I am not the Saviour,
nor even a saviour.
There are limits to what I can
do. Knowing my limits
means that within those
boundaries I can do the
maximum good.

Challenge

One man's defeat
is another man's challenge.

Did you expect to enjoy the
view at the top of the
mountain without developing
muscles on the climb?

A challenge does not
simply ask what we can do,
it asks who we are.

Performance

Anyone can boast of giving a
better performance – from the
spectator's stand.

It's strange how you can be
exhausted before commencing a
job that you hate or fear, and
full of energy once you have put
in the work to complete it.

Children

Put-downs do not help
a child grow up.

Ego trains her children for
dependence, in the guise of
motherly love, because she
needs to be needed. But
Wisdom trains her children for
independence, then finds they
come around for a chat anyway.

Children and God

If you want your children to
come openly and eagerly to God,
then by your welcoming arms
encourage them to come openly
and eagerly to you.

Children learn how to define
trust long before they can
spell the word.

Attention

A child who can maintain balance, and cycle alone, is not an insult to the parent but a living testament to their success.

Give your ears to the two-year-old and you will have a greater chance of catching the ears of the teen.

Opportunities

If you punish a child for
being honest, what options
does he have to protect himself
from your anger?

There is always the opportunity
to criticise, but not always the
opportunity to praise.
Grasp the chance to praise
whenever you can.

Confidence

Confidence is built on competence, not sweet talk. If you want confident children build their skills. Self-confidence will emerge as a by-product.

If we place our confidence in God, it's in safe keeping.

Courage

Courage means having a spirit
one step bigger than the
mountain you face.

Courage involves believing that
good will win, and you will be
there for the celebration.

Encourage!

To encourage is to fill another's
courage cup so they can drink.

Courage is optimism in action.
To act today you need to believe
that what you do now will make
a difference tomorrow.

War and peace

Cowardice today, war tomorrow.
Courage today, peace tomorrow.

This is a command to take to
heart: 'Have a strong and steady
courage. Whatever you do, don't
give in to fear, or bow to
discouragement. For the Lord
your God is with you wherever
you go.' *(See Joshua 1:9.)*

Stand up!

Courage is often the simple act
of standing up when you would
rather lie down with the rest.

Appeasement

Appeasement does not
buy you peace.
It simply increases the
likelihood of being beaten in a
future battle.

Desire

No one longs for what they already have, instead they take it for granted and stretch out for the mirage of better things just out of reach. Because they are busy looking over the fence, the relationships they already have may die from neglect, leaving them nothing.

One of the secrets of happiness, then, is to revel in present blessings.

'Godliness with contentment is great gain.'

(See 1 Timothy 6:6.)

Dreams

You may have to say 'No' to many fantasies in order to say 'Yes' to achieving one dream.

Saying 'No' will hurt, and there are seasons in life when you may need to grieve the loss of many dreams.

This will free you to focus your courage and time on living wholeheartedly one 'Yes!'

Focus

Those who hold tightly to all
their dreams may fail to achieve
one.

It takes longer to give birth
to a bigger baby and the same is
true of dreams!

Crossroads

A person who cannot decide which path to take will stick at the crossroads – and get run over.

Indecision is more tiring and expensive than investing in a course of action.

Vision

To have a bigger vision than
average is to risk more suffering
and struggle than average,
but at least you are alive from
the tips of your fingers to the
depths of your soul.

Discouragement

Discouragement simply means
that you have used up
all your courage.
You need a refill.

Result of chaos

Discouragement is, in some ways, the opposite of creation. God took chaos and made order and beauty out of it, but we see chaos and make a run for it.

Power within you

Discouragement involves an optical illusion, in which you see the problem before you as greater than the power that is within you.

Thankfulness

It takes fewer words to thank a
man for the lawn he's cut,
than it does to point out all
the grass he's missed.

I've heard it also takes fewer
muscles to smile than to frown.

Courtesy

I wonder how many relationships would be saved, and people encouraged, if we simply treated each other with the same courtesies we extend to strangers.

Criticism

Most of us doubt ourselves
enough without further
evidence being presented.

Try not to be the source of
another person's
discouragement by critical
comments and put-downs.

If you really feel you
have to say something
'for their own good,'
also give them a generous
serving of hope.

Losing control

People who attempt suicide do not usually want to die. In seeking an emotional painkiller they pick one with fatal side-effects.

Feeling out of control, they seek to have final control over something, but sadly end up losing all control.

Mountains and valleys

Either side of a mountain top experience there is a steep valley.

God knows!

Efficiency

At times it may be necessary to
be professional, maybe clinical,
but even a clinic can
have fragrant flowers in
the waiting room.

Inspiration

Efficiency does not spring from imposing regulations on people and tying them up in red tape against their wishes, but rather from collectively and individually educating, empowering and inspiring people to follow their hearts.

Fame

Fame is my needing you, lots of the time, to say that I am OK.

Fame, like an addiction, needs ever higher doses to be effective. Yet it does not cure the disease of low self-esteem.

If the fame fades, the fear re-emerges. What then?

Will the person display bizarre behaviour to gain more attention, or will they grow up?

Fear

If we put the 'fear of God' into
children, why are we so
surprised when they flee from
us,
and from God, as adults?

Until we face them, our fears
have free reign to shape us.

Love

Our lives tend to be driven by fear. As students we fear failing, as parents we fear the consequences of messing up our children, and as Christians we worship or confess our sins from fear of God. This makes us tense, intense and self-absorbed.

What would happen instead if we replaced all those fears with love?

Freedom

Freedom is like a fast car.
You need lessons before you
can drive it safely.

Some parents give lessons,
but never the car.
Others give the car,
but no lessons.

Glory

In our humanity we associate the idea of glory with showy display, yet when God revealed his glory to Moses it featured his mercy and grace.

God

The heart is a better means of measuring love than science will ever be. The same is true when it comes to God.

When it comes to salvation, 'courage' and 'surrender' can be used in the same sentence.

Habit

Good habits
economise
on will power.

Hate

As a Christian I am urged, for the health of my spirit and the good of the world, not to hate anyone or anything. Surely this includes refusing to hate myself, or any part of my body.

Just as I refuse to hate you, I refuse to hate myself.

Hate is blind

Hate can be as blind
as love any day.

In reality hate does not argue a
point, it simply seeks to crush
the other, body and soul. It is
prompted not by reason but by
revenge. It does not desire to
educate but to eliminate. Such
'holy' wars are played out in
living rooms across the nation,
as well as on the world stage.

The acid of hate

If I carry the acid of hate in order to splash it on someone, I end up corroding my own soul. If instead, I seek to understand my enemy and forgive, I in turn am healed.

Hope

Every now and again Courage climbs up and stands on the rock of Hope, and, looking into the distance, sees that today's actions will benefit and bless tomorrow. So it climbs down and, with the vision gained from Hope still firmly in mind, rolls up its sleeves and gets back to work.

Hoping

Hope for the best then relax and enjoy the picnic, knowing you have packed your raincoat.

To have hope does not mean to be blind to reality, but to believe that good is ultimately greater than evil, and that you can have a part in making that belief come true.

Losing hope

You lose hope when you forget
what you have already achieved.
It is not what you face that
daunts you, but doubt in your
own capacity to cope.
This doubt can be eased if you
recall all the times that you were
faced with a cold morning, or a
hard time, and you got up and
lived through it anyway.

Imagination

Imagination can create higher
mountains than it can climb.
On earth this may appear
to be a problem, but it is
merely a symptom
of our craving for eternity.

Friend or foe?

Imagination is the first step
towards any creation.

Imagination can be your foe or
your friend. It can cause you to
worry and think the worst,
and lead to the paralysing
belief that everyone and
everything is against you. . .

or it can lead you to look
ahead with hope, and see
visions of a stronger self and
the job accomplished.

Tame your imagination,
or it will rule you.

Dreams and elbow grease

It is fine for children to dream,
as long as they can also
roll up their sleeves.

The path to dreams
is made smoother
by applying elbow grease.

Castles in the air

By all means
build castles in the air,

but also study
for your builder's licence

so that you can construct
foundations under them.

Integrity

Integrity is more than honesty.
It involves having the courage to
live out your inner convictions,
to be true on the outside to the
best you are on the inside.

The greater your integration the
greater your peace – with others
and with yourself.

Integrity is more than skin
deep, it goes right to the back
bone.

Judging

Never judge a butterfly's
beauty and ability to fly by the
shape of the chrysalis.

We are all butterflies
in the making.

Love

Use things, love people.

To be 'in love' may simply mean
that we have at last found
someone who reflects our own
goodness back to us,
and so we feel worthy.

Dear God,

Please help my love
to be greater than their hate,

and your love
for me
to be greater than my sin.

In Jesus' name

Amen

Motivation

People will work harder and faster out of anticipation than out of gratitude.

Past success motivates present behaviour in anticipation of a future reward.

Don't nag!

Nagging is as exhausting as lifting someone else's legs to make them walk, so give the person who nags you a well-deserved break – stand on your own two feet!

Opportunities

Opportunities are just that.
They are not commanders,
nor are they servants.

They are invitations.

Master Time sets the deadline,
and you have the right of reply.

Trying to grasp every
opportunity means you risk
dropping them all.

Optimism

Bricklayers are
practical optimists.

With their eyes they may see a
pack of bricks but with their
heart they see a house. So, acting
on hope born of experience, they
lift the bricks one-by-one until
the job is done.

Optional extra

Optimism plants brown
bulbs in winter to pick bright
blooms in Spring.

Optimism is always optional.
Choosing your mood
is compulsory.

Optimism is right as often as
pessimism, but it laughs more
along the way.

Persistence

It may be great to start with the hardest job first, but often we lack both the energy and the willpower.

We don't need to succumb to inertia, though, for even at our lowest ebb we can still make a small start.

That's how a wedge begins its work – thin end first.

Small decisions

There is no need to fear persistence. All it involves is a series of small decisions to keep going, but it leads to great results.

Power

If you have power over another person and abuse it, when your power wanes your relationship will wane along with it.

But if you have power over another person and use it to empower them, they will grow strong in the skills needed to support you in your own time of weakness.

If power goes to your head, it leaves your heart.

Apathy

Passion and zeal always win
against apathy, whether
their cause is good or bad,
for apathy stays at home and
toasts its toes by the fire.

'Encourage one another
and build each other up.'

1 Thessalonians 5:11, NIV.

Resilience

Resilience involves using the energy generated by the put-down to bounce back.

Resilience and survival depend on our keeping flexible in joint and journey.

When to bend

Those who are resilient
know when to bend to the
will of the wild winds, and
when to bounce back.

Though great trees may crash
to earth, grass is greener
after the storm.

Resolution

Suppose today was New Year's
Day. What would you resolve?
What would you do?
Then do it, for today and every
day is New Year's Day.

Responsibility

Though we may want a bigger
serving of cake, we are always
willing for others to have a
bigger serving of responsibility.

Follow-through

To be responsible means we have both the skill to respond appropriately, and the will to follow through.

Fleeing from life

Those who flee from all
responsibility and depend on
others to rescue them, also flee
from managing, and therefore
relishing, their own lives.

Security

From birth we fear falling,
God knows. Falling down stairs,
falling out of love, falling from
grace, falling from high office,
falling into sin.

We hate the pain, humiliation,
injury and loss of control.

When we fall, sometimes a
person is there to catch us,
and at other times we feel
the full effect of gravity.

That's why God's promise
of a secure eternal life means
so much to us.

Self-discipline

Self-discipline involves
enlisting the law of cause and
effect on your side.

Self-discipline involves loving
your future self enough to curb
the desires of your present self

Self-leadership

When you are self-disciplined,
it means that you are a leader
whom you respect enough to
follow. You become a disciple of
your own higher self.

True self-discipline is more
friend and mentor than tyrant.

Direction

Self-discipline is what kicks in
when motivation goes on leave.

Lack of self-discipline involves
swapping present ease for
future pain and feeling
you've got a bargain.

Self-respect

When I view the world through lenses of low self-esteem, I see smiles distorted to smirks. And you wonder why I hide?

I respect myself when I do what I say I will do. I trust myself when I keep my promises to myself.

The gauge

I gauge respect for myself using
the same measure I use for
others. Do I keep my promises?
Do I act decisively?
Do I show kindness?
Have I got a strong
moral backbone?

Do I know how to use time and
love people? Am I honest to all,
and can I live with integrity?

The more I can say 'Yes'
to my own questions,
the more I respect myself.

Standing high

I stand high in my own regard if
I measure high on my own self–
imposed standards. There are
times when my behaviour needs
adjusting, and there are times
when my standards need
adjusting in the light of reality.

Self-esteem quotient

Like you, I have an inbuilt
surveillance system. It monitors
all I do, and measures it
against my self-made
standards of behaviour.

It then gives me feedback in
terms of a self-esteem quotient.
Some call it conscience.

Self-pity

People who wallow in self-pity are like jellyfish rising and falling with the waves. They always expect an external force to lift them and give them buoyancy. Their moods fluctuate wildly according to circumstance and, though others may try to support them, it's tiring work, so no one can do it for long.

Status

The lower people's social status,
the more respect we need to pay
them, because it is often their
labour that maintains our
status.

Standing tall

You cannot hold another man
down and stand tall yourself.

It is not wealth or height
or intelligence that gives
a person stature, but the
dignity of kindness.

Stress

The camel's back is not broken by the last straw, but by the bales that have been stored before.

Stress is like water exploring a crack in the dam.

Although it may target our weakest point, if we are aware of this we can know where to shore up our defences.

Stress limit

When you travel the road of life, it can be just as important not to exceed your stress limit, as not to exceed your alcohol limit.

'Greater is he who is in you than he who is in the world.' Jesus.

Magnifying troubles

Troubles, and magnifying
glasses, are best stored
separately.

Some attract stress.
Some create stress for others.
Some have stress thrust
upon them.
Some ride stress till it submits.
Others ease the stress of others.
Which are you?

Time

Why do we kill time,
begging for eternity?

Love is spelt T I M E.

When I give you some of my
time, I give you some of my life.

Deadlines

Deadlines can prove lifelines to
those who tend to procrastinate.

Time is a mortal measure.
The more mortal we feel,
the more we measure it.

Earth and Eternity

Earth: people bowing to the dictates of invisible Time, and questioning the reality of God.

Eternity: people bowing to a visible God, and ignoring Time completely.

Storing time

Money can be hoarded and spent. Time can be saved and spent, yet nowhere can it be stored.

If you lose time, it hides and can never be found. Maybe somewhere there is a place where all the lost hours go, next-door to the final resting place of lost socks and lost pens.

Time spent enriches the simplest gift.

Time spent

To get your work done, either spend your time, or spend money buying another's time.

An old person is just someone who has had lots of time in readiness for eternity. A young person is someone who feels immortal already.

Enjoy the journey

Time is like a suitcase that fills
too quickly. Contented people
are those who have learned what
to pack into time to travel light,
and so enjoy the journey.

Will power

Many tire themselves out
drawing on their will power
when 'want' power would take
them there with ease.

`Want' power

Using will power to pull against won't power is like having a tug of war in your mind. No one goes anywhere and everyone ends up sore and exhausted. Instead, focus on want power.

Worry

Worry is reaching out with
your heart when your
arms are too short.

Worry is fear out on parole.

Worry changes nothing

Worry wearies the soul without
changing it. Only thoughts
that turn into actions
change situations.

Worry exhausts itself riding a
rocking horse faster and
faster under the illusion that
it is gallantly galloping
to save someone.

You

What are you waiting for?
For rescue?

It is within your hands to dust
yourself off, to rise from the
mud of defeat and take a
shower.

For permission? You had it from
your first breath.

For a clear path ahead? Such
paths do not exist, just take the
best path you can find, and
begin to walk along it.

Live a little

Dare to live a little, to follow
your dreams, to put your
best foot forward.

An act of courage,
however small, is a vote of
confidence in the future.

Selfishness

Selfishness springs from
emptiness and fear.

This occurs when the black hole
within each person consumes all
the attention it is fed, and
demands more.

By contrast, God is the Source
of all life and at his centre is a
spring of eternal life which
overflows in acts of love.

Sin

Sin is what we call annoying
behaviour in someone else.

Sin is our mortal attempt to
patch the life-leak where we
have torn away from God.

Sin is me thinking of me and
forgetting God has already
thought of me and I have no
need to worry.

Sin is also

Me trying to force my way into
the limelight, when God has
already offered me the Son
in my heart.

If we recognise that everyone's a
bit cracked we'll be less
surprised when they show a few
fault lines.

Righteousness

If we abandon the robe of our own self-righteousness, people may more readily recognise us as fellow human beings.

Then we can share with them the knowledge of God's righteousness.

To be made right we first have to admit we are in the wrong.

Eden's gates

When God closed the gates of
Eden he not only barred us from
the Tree of Life, but from
perfection. Often, we waste
time and effort trying to prise
those golden gates open, but
only God has the power to
reopen
what he has closed. That is why
God, in Jesus, is the only Way to
life and perfection.

Perfection

It is true that Jesus commands us to be perfect, but he did not say this to increase the speed of our halo polishing, but rather to urge us to forget ourselves in acts of kindness.

When we do, the world will truly catch a glimpse of God's perfect character and grace.

See Matthew 5:43-48.

The search

A craftsman who loves what he is making unconsciously seeks perfection. Ultimately, then, perfection is not about fear but about love.

To throw one's whole heart into learning how to love: that is to seek perfection.

Pride

In polishing our pedestals of pride, we easily become self-absorbed, self-centred and critical of those who appear to get in our way. This is the exact opposite of godliness.

The measurement

Have you ever given or received the perfect hug? Who can tell? There are no rules to measure hugs. Just as a hug transcends rules, love fulfils the law of God by transcending it.

Relationships

In human relationships
harmony may sometimes be
maintained by making no sound
at all – while biting on your
tongue!

If you see every person as your
teacher you will be quicker to
listen and slower to condemn.

Religion

People of all religions bark.
Some are just
'barking up the wrong tree.'

The desire for life and
immortality is universal, so,
therefore, is the seeking.
Our differences lie simply
in the methods we use and what,
or who, we find.

The weight of a smile

People join or leave religious systems for four main reasons:

to feed their physical, spiritual, social and mental needs.

There are those who come, and those who go, because of the doctrine that is taught, but most change churches for emotional rather than religious reasons.

That's why a smile can carry more weight than a sermon.

Perfect church

The perfect church
would be empty.

Religion does not save us.
It is merely a description
of the One who does.

Religion is often a gathering
together of the vulnerable
seeking the Able.

Problem solved

You can come into the kitchen now: the dishes have been done. You can come to God now: the sin problem has been solved.

Standards

Before raising the standards,
energise the people.

In the Christian life, love leaps
higher than fear.

Do we try to achieve standards,
or do we bear the standard of
Jesus before us? What is the
difference?

Setting the standards

Who has set or imposed your standards? What guidelines did they use, and how do you measure for yourself if they are fair?

Christian standards are not for jumping, they are for carrying.

Tyrants & Tyranny

Faint hearts make stepping-stones for tyrants.

If a tyrant's policy is 'divide and conquer', the policy of the people needs to be 'unite and thrive'.

Bullies and victims

Each act of appeasement progressively strengthens the bully and weakens the victim.

Tyranny breeds liars, for it is fear that speaks. We lie most to those we fear most, and we fear most those who can hurt us or judge us most. In contrast, perfect love drives out fear. Honest to God.

Walking

Those who stand still may seem more secure than those who walk, but it is those who walk who develop spiritual muscles and find new horizons of the spirit.

Whenever you walk you alternate between stability and instability. The same is true of walking by faith. There are times when you are sure of everything, and times when you are sure of nothing.

Witnessing

Every Christian is a Bible translator – some even use words.

All human beings have a wealthy Father. Christians know of this inheritance and missionaries are couriers bearing the Good News of it to all parts of the world.

Worry

It is a natural instinct for most of us to make molehills into mountains, and then try to climb them. Worry may be natural, but it is also optional.

By all means plan for tomorrow, but don't worry about it. Enjoy living in the present.

See Matthew 6:33, 34.

You

You are part of the Family of God, with the same surname as Jesus, so take on this identity fully, and stand strong in him. Open your heart to the love of God and feel yourself being filled to overflowing with his Spirit. Then everyone will see the glorious character of God and his grace revealed through you.

See Ephesians 3:14-21.